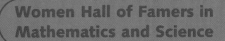

Gertrude Elion

Nobel Prize Winner in
Physiology and Medicine

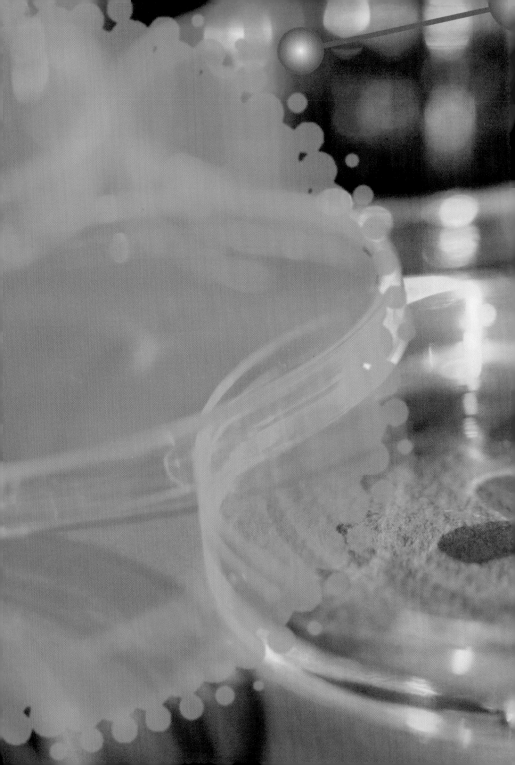

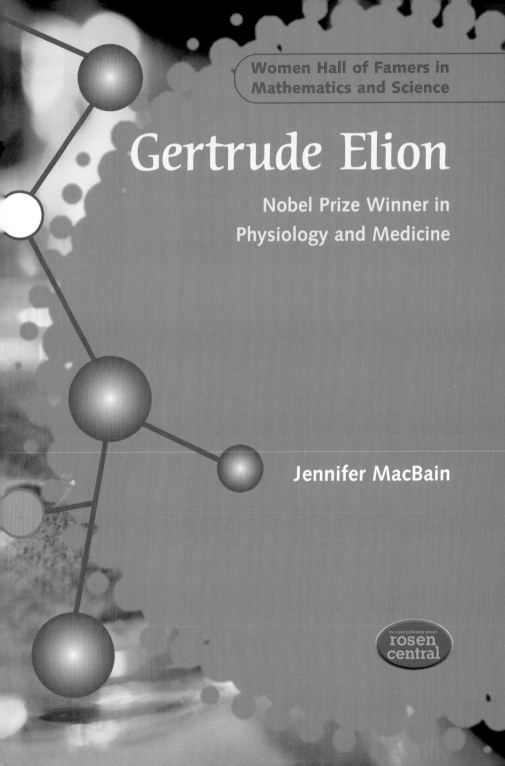

Gertrude Elion

Nobel Prize Winner in
Physiology and Medicine

Jennifer MacBain

the rosen publishing group's
rosen
central

For my grandfather, Dr. Philip Weiss

Published in 2004 by The Rosen Publishing Group, Inc.
29 East 21st Street, New York, NY 10010

First Edition

Library of Congress Cataloging-in-Publication Data

MacBain, Jennifer.
Gertrude Elion : Nobel prize winner in physiology and medicine / by Jennifer MacBain.— 1st ed.
    p. cm. — (Women hall of famers in mathematics and science)
Summary: A biography of the woman who used her understanding of chemistry to help develop medicines and who devoted her life to helping others.
Includes bibliographical references and index.
ISBN 0-8239-3876-X
1. Elion, Gertrude B.—Juvenile literature. 2. Pharmacologists— United States—Biography—Juvenile literature. 3. Women medical scientists—United States—Biography—Juvenile literature. 4. Nobel Prizes—Biography—Juvenile literature. [1. Elion, Gertrude B. 2. Chemists. 3. Scientists. 4. Women—Biography. 5. Nobel Prizes— Biography.] I. Title. II. Series.
RM62.E43 M33 2003
615'.19'0092—dc21

                                    2002011375

Manufactured in the United States of America

Contents

Introduction 7

1 **Coming to New York** 12

2 **College and Beyond** 23

3 **In the Lab** 35

4 **Helping the Innocent** 48

5 **Continuing to Cure** 61

6 **Retired and Rewarded** 71

7 **Looking Back** 87

Timeline 96

Glossary 99

For More Information 102

For Further Reading 105

Bibliography 106

Index 108

Introduction

From the time that Gertrude Elion was a young girl, she enjoyed discovering new things. She wanted to follow in the footsteps of the female scientist Marie Curie, whose research earned her two Nobel Prizes—in 1903 for physics and in 1911 for chemistry. Curie's remarkable achievements paved the way for other women scientists, including Gertrude. Young Gertrude didn't know it at the time, but she, too, would become well known for her scientific research and discoveries, namely her work in the field of medicine. And she would also be rewarded with a Nobel Prize, just like Marie Curie.

In the lab, Gertrude was a hard worker. She helped to develop six different drugs used to combat nine serious medical conditions, including leukemia, malaria, viral herpes, and AIDS. She also worked to develop a drug that would make organ transplants possible by forcing patients' bodies to accept transplanted organs. Her work was groundbreaking, and her medicines are still in use today. But Gertrude always considered herself to be more of a humanist than a scientist. Her life was devoted to helping others, and although she was often rewarded with various honors, she didn't need them to feel like she had achieved great things. Her prized treasures were not the awards and medals she won through the academic circuit but the many letters from parents of children who expressed unending appreciation for the medicines she created. They thanked her for saving the lives of their loved ones.

Gertrude had personal reasons for choosing the career path of a pharmacologist—a person who studies the science of medicines, including how they act and react with each other. She faced several personal tragedies when people she loved died before their time. First, her beloved grandfather died a painful death from stomach cancer in 1933. Then, Gertrude's fiancé, the love of her life, died of a disease that would have been easily cured today with the help of medicines like the ones Gertrude helped to create. And finally, J. B., a patient to whom Gertrude grew close while treating her for leukemia, died after a period of time believing she was cured for life. These horrible instances fueled Gertrude's desire to find medicines that would help cure people of deadly diseases.

At a young age, Gertrude desperately wanted to help people, but at that time women were expected to become nurses and teachers, not research chemists. This all changed, however, in 1941, when the United States entered World War II. Many American men were called away to serve in the war. The women who were left behind had to go to work, not just working as nurses or teachers but in many different, varied fields, taking the place of the men who were fighting overseas.

It was Dr. George Hitchings who gave Gertrude a chance at a career in medicine. Dr. Hitchings, head of the biochemistry department at Burroughs Wellcome, a company that made pharmaceuticals, liked Gertrude's ambition and intelligence, and he gave her a job. Suddenly, Gertrude had a real opportunity to learn and grow as an assistant biochemist. Even without an advanced degree in her field, she worked her way up the corporate ladder and in the laboratory. She had her first breakthrough at the age of thirty-two, when she created a drug that, with the use of other drugs, would eventually create a beneficial treatment for childhood leukemia. Through the years, Gertrude had many other breakthroughs at Burroughs Wellcome. She was eventually promoted to head of the Department of Experimental Therapy—a great honor, considering she was the first female to lead such a department. By this time, the company had become one of the world's leading pharmaceutical companies.

Throughout her life, Gertrude remained hard working and inquisitive. She was known for her work ethic and the fact that she was always asking questions. People knew her to be a workaholic, but she enjoyed life as well. She loved photography and was quoted in a 1993 interview with the *Tampa Tribune* as saying, "I'll climb a mountain to get a picture." When she wasn't traveling to Asia or South America for vacation, she was attending operas with friends at the Metropolitan Opera House in New York City and collecting artwork to fill her two-story condominium in North Carolina. Gertrude loved life and proved to be a dedicated spirit in helping others until the day she died.

Coming to New York

According to a lecture at Wakefield Forest University entitled "Judaism in America," two million Jews immigrated to America between 1870 and 1914. Many of these Jews fled persecution in Russia and the Austro-Hungarian Empire. (The Austro-Hungarian Empire is now split up into individual countries, such as the Czech Republic, Austria, Hungary, and Slovakia.) The governments of these countries took away basic rights of different ethnic groups and eventually set them apart by putting them in poor ghetto areas. Jews came to America so they could practice their religious beliefs in peace and to escape persecution.

During World War I (1914–1918), 100,000 more came, and by 1924, 250,000 Jews had arrived in the United States. Many of these immigrants were peasants rather than businessmen. Less than 6 percent of Russian immigrants brought more than $50 with them. Many of these Jewish people settled in New York City. At one time, New York contained half of all the Jews in the country. Their first task was to find work.

A DENTIST AND A SEAMSTRESS

Robert Elion was twelve years old when he came to America from Lithuania, a country located to the northeast of Poland. He eventually came to work nights in a drugstore so that he could save up enough money to go to college. He finally saved up to attend New York University's School of Dentistry, from which he graduated in 1914. He married Bertha Cohen, a young seamstress, when she was only nineteen years old. Bertha had come to America from Poland when she was fourteen. Robert and Bertha started off in a large New York City apartment that doubled as Robert's dental

Gertrude's mother, Bertha, pictured here with Gertrude in 1921, impressed upon her daughter that having a career of her own was very important. Gertrude far surpassed her mother's expectations in her lifetime. Bertha would have been very proud to see her daughter win the Nobel Prize.

office. Eventually, Robert had several dental offices, and he invested in stocks and real estate.

Their red-haired daughter, Gertrude Belle Elion, was born January 23, 1918, on a night so cold that the pipes in their apartment froze and burst. Luckily, the family was busy in the hospital, welcoming their new baby into the family. Everyone called her Trudy. When Trudy was seven, the family moved to the Bronx, where she attended public school. As a child, Trudy loved going to the Bronx Zoo and playing in the open parks. From the age of ten, Trudy went with her father to the Metropolitan Opera House to see operas and listen to music. This began a tradition that Trudy would follow into adulthood. She learned to love music.

Robert was known as a wise man: He was descended from a line of rabbis, or leaders of Jewish congregations, and fellow immigrants sought his advice on problems. He always wanted to travel more but never seemed to be able to get away. Instead, he showed Trudy various train maps and bus schedules, planning imaginary trips.

Bertha, too, came from a scholarly family. Her grandfather had been a scholar in her community. It was a custom for Russian Jews to first send their eldest child to America to get established, and then the younger ones would arrive later. So when Bertha first came to New York, she stayed with her older sisters. She attended night school to learn English and worked in the garment trade. Bertha was intelligent and had great common sense. As Trudy grew up, Bertha urged her daughter to find a career so she would have money to spend on things she wanted. Like many wives at that time, Bertha had to justify to her husband every cent she spent. According to *Nobel Prize Women in Science* by Sharon Bertsch McGrayne, Gertrude remembered, "Getting a little extra money [from her father] was like filing a new grant application. You had to have an explanation, and you had to essentially go begging for it. You couldn't just go out and buy something."

TRUDY'S CHILDHOOD

As a child, Trudy had a huge thirst for knowledge. It didn't matter if the subject was history, foreign languages, or science—Trudy was like a sponge absorbing information. She loved to read about anything and everything, especially books pertaining to her two favorite idols, Marie Curie and Louis Pasteur. Marie Curie was considered to be one of the greatest scientists of this century. Her studies contributed profoundly to our current understanding of radioactivity. Louis Pasteur made the discovery that most infectious diseases are caused by germs. This

One of Gertrude's idols as a child was Marie Curie, two-time winner of the Nobel Prize, and the first woman to win the award. Marie, like Gertrude, was encouraged by her family to learn and to get an education. Both women enjoyed great success and acclaim for their scientific research.

is known as the germ theory of disease, one of the most important breakthroughs in medical history. Trudy's favorite book was Paul de Kruif's *Microbe Hunters*, an international best-seller that illustrates the achievements and mistakes of early microbiologists. The book explores the work of various scientists, doctors, and medical technicians that led to the understanding of various diseases and cures.

It wasn't just a love of learning that made Trudy's childhood enjoyable. When Trudy was three years old, her grandfather emigrated from Russia. As she grew up with him living in the house, she developed a close, loving bond with him. Her grandfather was a watchmaker and a

learned scholar. He spoke several languages, including Yiddish. As he got older, his eyesight faded and instead of repairing watches, he enjoyed taking long walks with Trudy in the park, telling her stories, and speaking Yiddish with her.

In 1924, Gertrude's brother, Herbert, was born. As children they were slightly competitive and enjoyed teasing each other. Herbert often played practical jokes on Trudy. For example, when Trudy got older and brought boyfriends home, Herbert would turn the lights out on them. Until Trudy won the Nobel Prize, it was Herbert that the family considered the "smart child." Herbert eventually majored in engineering in college and went

THE GREAT DEPRESSION

The stock market crash of 1929 was the beginning of the Great Depression in America. In early 1929, when President Herbert Hoover was ushered into office, there was a feeling of optimism throughout the country and the illusion of stability. When the depression hit, it was considered the worst economic slump in United States history. Eventually, the slump spread to the rest of the world.

Continued on page 20

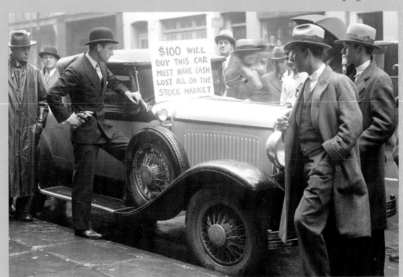

The stock market crash of 1929 had a severe impact on the economy of the United States. Here, a man tries to sell his car to earn some money.

Continued from page 19

Many factors contributed to the Great Depression, but one of the main reasons was the unequal distribution of wealth in the country. There was a vast difference between the rich and the working-class people. This created an unstable economy.

The depression created a slew of problems. Many people lost their jobs. The number of high school dropouts rose as many students struggled to help their families. The rate of homelessness also rose, and people started to protest. Farmers began arming themselves with guns and pitchforks to march on the banks and prevent foreclosures.

on to own a bio-engineering and communications engineering firm.

As youngsters, Gertrude and Herbert did not have the financial struggles they would experience later. It wasn't until 1929 that the Elion family began struggling with their finances. Before this time, Robert's dental practices and investments ensured their financial stability.

EARLY SIGNS OF A BRIGHT FUTURE

By the time Gertrude was twelve, her intelligence was apparent. She was able to skip two grades in school and graduate from high school at the age of fifteen. Unfortunately, the United States was in the midst of an economic crisis. A year earlier, when Gertrude was eleven, the stock market crashed. Robert Elion, who had invested heavily in the stock market, was forced to declare bankruptcy. Declaring bankrupcty meant that the Elion family was financially ruined. The money they once had was gone. Luckily the family got by because Robert still had his dental practice and loyal customers. The family had no money to send Gertrude to college, however. She had to find her own way to pay her tuition.

According to *Nobel Prize Women in Science*, Gertrude said, "Among immigrant Jews, their one way to success was education . . . The person you admired most was the person with the most education. And particularly because I was the firstborn, and I loved school, and I was good in school, it was obvious that I should go on with my education. No one ever dreamt of not going to college."

Fortunately, Gertrude's grades were very good and Hunter College, the women's branch of the City College of New York, had free tuition in 1933. Gertrude was accepted and decided to take advantage of the free tuition. If they had charged tuition as they do today, Gertrude would not have been able to attend.

2

College and Beyond

Gertrude enrolled at Hunter College in 1933, at the age of fifteen. Gertrude's brother, Herbert, would also enroll for free at the College of the City of New York and study physics and engineering. Gertrude truly enjoyed going to school. In her autobiography on the Nobel e-Museum Web site (http://www.nobel.se), she said, "I remember my school days as being very challenging and full of good comradery among the students. It was an all-girls school and I think many of our teachers were uncertain whether most of us would really go on with our careers. As a matter of fact, many of the girls went on to become teachers and some went into scientific research."

TAKING INSPIRATION FROM SADNESS

Gertrude's father wanted her to study dentistry or perhaps medicine, but Gertrude knew that studying biology would involve dissecting things in the lab, and she did not want to do such a thing. Her other teachers hoped she would pursue their subject matters, like English or even French. But it was the death of Gertrude's beloved grandfather that inspired her to major in chemistry. She watched him die slowly and painfully of stomach cancer in 1933. Gertrude was the apple of her grandfather's eye, and she was deeply affected by his death. According to the New Jersey Association for Biomedical Research, she said, "He was taken to the hospital and, after a while, I was allowed to visit him. Seeing him there, I remember how shocked I was at his change in appearance. It was the first time I really understood how awful disease could be. I wondered how this happened to people. In the hope that I could do something to combat disease, I decided to become a scientist."

In 1937, Gertrude graduated from Hunter College with high honors. Had it not been for financial hardship, she would have gone on to graduate school right away. Instead, Gertrude spent some time working and saving money to be able to afford graduate school.

It was then that Gertrude focused all her energies on chemistry, and she loved what she studied. She found the environment at Hunter stimulating, and she never looked back. Though there were seventy-five chemistry majors in her class, most of these young women would end up teaching it—but Gertrude wanted to do research. Luckily, she learned about new discoveries from one special professor, Dr. Otis, who arranged a study group for women who wanted to become serious scientists. The young women met at Dr. Otis's home and discussed articles from scholarly journals he gave them. The interest that he showed in his pupils would make a lasting impression on Gertrude. In later years, she tried to give this kind of attention to the students in her classes.

In 1937, Gertrude graduated with a bachelor's of science degree in chemistry. She graduated Phi Beta Kappa and summa cum laude (with highest honors). Phi Beta Kappa is considered to be the most prestigious honor society in the nation. A student must be elected to the society, and this is done after completing ninety-six school credits in only three years. Gertrude was a member.

PAYING HER OWN WAY

Anxious to pursue work in pharmaceutical research, for which she would eventually need a doctorate degree, she applied to fifteen graduate schools. Though her grades were superb, all of them turned her down for financial aid or assistantships. And she could not even find a job to pay her own way due to the ongoing economic crisis. When she got an interview to work in a laboratory, she was told she was qualified but she was too pretty and would be a distracting influence on the men in the lab.

"I almost fell apart," Gertrude stated in *Nobel Prize Women in Science.* "That was the first time that I thought being a woman was a real disadvantage. It surprises me to this day that I didn't get angry. I got very discouraged."

From 1937 to 1944, Gertrude worked many different jobs. First she went to secretarial school but stayed for only six weeks. She dropped out to take a job teaching biochemistry to nurses at New York Hospital's School of Nursing. The position was unpaid and lasted for only three months, but Gertrude wanted the experience. From 1938 to 1939, she worked at the Denver Chemical Company in New York, sometimes having to endure anti-Semitic jokes, or jokes that imply a hatred of Jewish people. By the end of the year, she was paid $20 per week. She began to save this money for graduate school. Because she also lived at home, she was able to save a total of $450, enough for one year of graduate school. Her parents were also able to help her a bit with the cost of her tuition. She enrolled at New York University (NYU) in the fall of 1939. From 1940 to 1942, she made extra money by working as a permanent substitute chemistry and physics teacher in New York City high schools, making $7.50 a day. She worked during the day and went to school at night. Sometimes she worked in the lab on weekends, where the heat was turned down so low that she had to wear her winter coat and turn on the Bunsen burners for heat.

As a substitute teacher, Gertrude was barely older than the students in her physics class, so it was no surprise that she was subject to their scrutiny and practical jokes. One student in partic-ular was especially focused on making Gertrude feel bad. He tried to stump her with a physics question he had gotten from his college-age brother who was a physics major. When Gertrude answered his question without hesitating, the stu-dent was shocked.

ANOTHER LOVE LOST

Gertrude was the only woman in her graduating class of 1941. Along with this wonderful high, however, came a terrible low. It was during her graduate school years that Gertrude met the love

CORRECTING THE PROFESSOR

Dr. Philip Weiss, head of the polymers department at General Motors Research Laboratories in Michigan for twenty-two years, remembers going to school with Gertrude Elion. Dr. Weiss got his master's degree in physical chemistry at New York University at the same time as Gertrude. They met around 1940. In an interview given in April 2002, Dr. Weiss recalled:

> She was a very bright girl. In addition to having good grades, she always looked one step further to find information. I remember a specific example of her thirst for knowledge. We were taking a course in the chemistry of natural products. It was taught by a visiting professor. The professor gave us a multi-step synthesis for the creation of vitamin A. (This is when I start with a compound and I keep converting it to something until I have the compound of vitamin A.) In the steps that the professor gave us, Gertrude noticed that the conversion did not

Continued on page 30

Continued from page 29

work out. It was impossible to create vitamin A with the reagents the professor gave us. She went to the chemistry literature in the library and looked up the original synthesis of vitamin A and discovered that the reagents used were completely different than the ones the professor had given us. She told all of us the correct reagents to use for the exam. When we got the exams back, however, we got ten points off on that question. Gertrude felt this was not right. She and another student decided to see the professor—they even showed him the literature from the library. He said, "When I give you the synthesis for vitamin A, whether it is right or wrong, you are supposed to give me what I told you." They eventually just said "thank you," not wanting to be failed, and left.

Dr. Weiss does not believe that this professor lasted for more than another year at NYU. Even back then, Gertrude was questioning and looking for the truth in science, not to mention dealing with unpleasant people!

of her life, Leonard Canter. Leonard was a brilliant statistics major at City College. He studied abroad and planned on working at Merrill Lynch, an investment bank, after he graduated. When he returned from abroad, he and Gertrude planned to marry. But their plans were ruined in 1941 when Leonard died of subacute bacterial endocarditis, a strep infection of the heart valves and heart lining. Two years later, penicillin for this infection was created, which would have cured him immediately. It would have saved his life.

Gertrude was devastated. In *Nobel Prize Women in Science*, Gertrude's brother, Herbert, notes, "It was a heartbreaker and she never fully recovered . . . No one could match up to Leonard. And then, as it was more and more in the past, he became more and more bigger than life, and so the memory was just enshrined."

It was then that Gertrude gave up on the idea of marriage. All of her relatives wanted her to find someone else, but Gertrude did not. Her parents never bothered her about it, however. They just left her alone. Her loss just reinforced her

Gertrude and her fiancé, Leonard Canter, are pictured here in 1940. His death in 1941 was devastating for Gertrude, and she never married. Instead, she pushed herself even harder to find cures for diseases. Shortly after Leonard's death, a medicine that would have cured him was invented.

decision to help people through science. According to *Journeys of Women in Science and Engineering: No Universal Constants*, Gertrude said, "I never intended not to get married...This was also a time when women couldn't have both a family and a career very easily. I don't think that's true now. I see women who have both. In those days it would have been very much frowned on for a married woman to be working, or to come back to the lab if she had a child." She chose her career over the possibility of having a husband and children. Her dedication to work meant that she spent long hours at the lab and devoted most of her time and energy to her research. Gertrude, later, jokingly referred to her discovered compounds as her "children." Luckily for the Elion family, they were a close-knit group, and Gertrude was very close to Herbert's children. Although they did not always live physically close to one another, the distance did not strain their relationship.

WORKING THROUGH HER SORROW

After Gertrude's terrible loss, she threw herself into her work. In 1942, she finally found a legitimate lab job as a food chemistry analyst at the Quaker Maid Company, at the time a division of A&P. According to Tom Brokaw's book, *The Greatest Generation*, Gertrude said, "I tested the acidity of pickles, the mold in the frozen strawberries; I checked the color of egg yolk going into the mayonnaise. It wasn't exactly what I had in mind but it was a step in the right direction."

After a year and a half of dealing with pickles, moldy strawberries, and egg yolks, Gertrude was anxious to find a research job that pertained to more serious matters. She liked her job in the lab but had learned all she could from that one place. She wasn't utilizing her education to the best of her abilities, and she wanted to be doing work that benefited more people. She needed to move on. Before she left, she thanked her bosses for the opportunity they had given her and adopted the famous motto of Admiral David Glasgow Farragut, naval commander for the Union (United States) in the Civil War (1861–1865), "Damn the torpedoes! Full speed ahead!"

3

In the Lab

After finding a promising job at Johnson & Johnson, manufacturers of health-care products, Gertrude was dismayed when the lab disbanded after six months. In 1944, Gertrude's father received a sample of the painkiller Empirin at his dental office from the pharmaceutical company Burroughs Wellcome (now called GlaxoSmithKline). He suggested Gertrude inquire about a job there. Gertrude didn't think the company had a research laboratory but decided to make the call anyway. When the receptionist answered, she explained that Gertrude could simply come in on Saturday. After having struggled just to get interviewed in the

A group of new draft inductees for World War II prepare to be marched to the checking station to receive their uniforms and equipment. Because the onset of World War II involved over one million men in the war effort, chemical laboratories were eager to hire female scientists.

past, Gertrude was amazed that this time she could just walk through the door!

Gertrude interviewed one week after D-Day (June 6, 1944), when more than one million men instantly went into uniform, even men who normally wore lab coats. These men were being sent to fight in World War II, and a lot of jobs opened up. Many chemists were called away to work for the war effort. The United States government exempted many chemistry students from the draft if they worked on defense projects. The scientists who worked for the war effort were not just expected to build a better tank. Among their tasks were to find a substitute for rubber (a supply that was cut off), to develop a new drug to fight malaria, and finally, to build an atomic bomb. This research demanded the attention of thousands of scientists. The National Defense Research Committee was formed to recruit scientists and oversee these projects.

NEW WOMAN AT WORK

Dr. George Hitchings, impressed with Gertrude's intelligence and verve, hired her on the spot as an assistant biochemist for $50 a week, a pretty good salary at that time. According to *Nobel Prize Women in Science*, Hitchings said, "She wanted fifty dollars a week. I thought she was worth it." This relationship would change both of their lives. She began working there at the age of twenty-six and would spend the next thirty-nine years of her life there. Gertrude never felt she had to move on because

Gertrude worked at Burroughs Wellcome (now GlaxoSmithKline) for thirty-nine years. During her time there, she became very close with many of her coworkers, including Dr. George Hitchings, with whom she shared a Nobel Prize after collaborating for many years.

she was constantly learning new things, moving from one field to another. Among the fields she mastered were organic chemistry (a branch of chemistry relating to carbon compounds), bio-chemistry (which deals with processes in living animals), pharmacology (the science of drugs), immunology (the science that deals with the immune system), and virology (the branch of sci-ence that deals with viruses). Gertrude stayed interested in her work, in part because of the many subjects she was able to learn about and study.

Founded in England in 1880 by two American pharmacists, Burroughs Wellcome was the offshoot of a British company set up by a char-itable trust, or an organization that is specifically set up to do charitable works. Silas Burroughs and Henry Wellcome were men who strove to bring a human side to science. Henry Wellcome wanted his scientists to have the freedom to pursue ideas. He wanted to focus on finding cures for serious, typically incurable diseases. Gertrude was an ideal worker for Burroughs Wellcome because she, too, believed in the humanistic side of science, and she

A photograph taken in 1948 shows Gertrude and Dr. Hitchings working in a laboratory at Burroughs Wellcome. Their goal was to develop a drug that would disable the cells diseased by cancer, bacteria, or viruses without harming the normal ones.

grew to become very interested in finding medicines to cure illnesses.

Though the main branch of the company was located in England, Gertrude would work in the laboratory in Tuckahoe, New York, about eight miles outside of New York City.

LIFE AT THE LAB

When Gertrude first set foot in the lab at Burroughs Wellcome, she saw one other woman

A SERIOUS MENTOR

Dr. George Hitchings, who one day would share the Nobel Prize with Gertrude, was born in Hoquiam, Washington, in 1905. After moving around quite a bit in his childhood, he was deeply impacted by the death of his father when he was twelve years old. This turned his attention toward medicine. He entered the University of Washington as a premed student but switched to chemistry and graduated with academic distinction in 1927. He eventually did graduate work at Harvard University and taught at Cambridge. He earned his Ph.D. in 1933 and married an artist, Beverly Reimer, with whom he had two children. His career slowed down in the 1930s during the depression, and he worked several jobs. Hitchings became head of the biochemistry department at Burroughs Wellcome in 1942.

Hitchings worked with Gertrude at Burroughs Wellcome to create several antiviral drugs. Their work made impressive steps toward curing childhood leukemia. At the beginning, the staff at

Continued on page 42

Continued from page 41

Burroughs Wellcome was small, and Hitchings and Gertrude worked continuously with each other. He was a mentor and was also impressed with her ability to learn. Sometimes their relationship was rocky. Gertrude once said Hitchings could be a little "patronizing." They had a very successful partnership, despite such things, and they continued to spur each other on.

Gertrude and Dr. George Hitchings are pictured here in 1988.

(out of a staff of seventy-five) in a lab coat. She immediately knew she could work there. This other woman was Elvira Falco, who originally did not want Hitchings to hire Gertrude because she was "dressed too nicely"; she didn't think Gertrude would get her hands dirty. (Gertrude had put on her best suit and hat for this interview!) Elvira and Gertrude ended up becoming great friends and attended operas together in New York City for years to come. (Gertrude's favorite operas were by Verdi, Puccini, and Mozart.) Although, when Gertrude crashed her car into a lamp post with Elvira in the passenger seat, Elvira did not want to drive with her again. Years later, Gertrude would also become very close with Hitchings's wife and children and would often visit them in North Carolina.

The conditions of the laboratory were not great. Dr. Hitchings, Gertrude, Elvira, and a British chemist named Peter Russell shared a large room without air-conditioning. A baby-food plant downstairs dehydrated food 365 days a year and the lab's floor would become very hot—over 140 degrees

Fahrenheit (60 degrees Celsius)! Gertrude wore very thick, rubber-soled nurses shoes to withstand the heat.

Despite the heat and cramped conditions, life was enjoyable in the laboratory. Elvira and Peter would get into water fights, and Peter told dirty jokes that made Gertrude blush. Gertrude was down to earth and unpretentious, and could concentrate "like a male," said Elvira, according to *Nobel Prize Women in Science*. Gertrude was allowed a lot of freedom when she began her work with Dr. Hitchings. Her first work was making compounds in the lab and seeing how they reacted when she placed them with leukemia cells. Would the leukemia cells use these compounds to help them multiply? Or would the compounds prevent the leukemia cells from invading more cells and growing? The interaction of these compounds could be seen under a microscope.

STILL CRAVING ACADEMIA

Although Gertrude was enjoying her time in the lab, she still wanted to go back to school to earn a

Ph.D. She began to take classes at Brooklyn's Polytechnic Institute but ran into an obstacle. She was informed that in order to continue in school, she would have to give up her part-time status and start taking classes full-time—a change that would prevent her from keeping her job at Burroughs Wellcome. But Gertrude did not want to give up her job in the lab. Her research was too important to her. In the end, she decided to stay with Burroughs Wellcome and give up her chance at a Ph.D. Years later, Gertrude received many honorary degrees, each of which helped her realize she had made the right decision to leave school and pursue her career as a scientist.

A NEW WAY OF DISCOVERING

Instead of the usual trial-and-error method in a lab, Dr. Hitchings and Gertrude developed a whole new process to research and create new drugs. They rationalized that all cells need nucleic acids to reproduce. Nucleic acids are the complex chemicals that genes are made of. One of the first things Gertrude worked on was the nucleic acids of DNA.

HONORARY DEGREES

An honorary degree is a degree given to a person by a university or college to honor that person for his or her work in a particular field. From 1969 on, Gertrude received three honorary doctorates from universities and twenty various other honorary degrees, including one from Harvard University in Massachusetts.

Dr. Hitchings knew that the cells of bacteria and tumors require large amounts of nucleic acids to sustain growth, much more than other cells. He realized these bad, bacterial substances would be very vulnerable to any disruption in their life cycle. Hence, Dr. Hitchings set up his assistants to try to disrupt the bacterial substances' cycles. They were going to find cures for diseases. Each study Gertrude embarked upon was like a mystery waiting to be solved. The work was fascinating to her.

Gertrude was happy to work long hours, never really satisfied until she had explored hundreds of variations of chemicals and figured out how they acted. Gertrude often took her work home with her. Within two years, Gertrude started publishing all of her findings. Eventually, she published more than 225 papers and Dr. Hitchings let her put her name first—a big deal since she was still technically his assistant and other people on the team had contributed their findings. It was only a matter of time before she had her first spectacular breakthrough that would save thousands of lives.

4

Helping the Innocent

Gertrude and Dr. Hitchings set out to disrupt the life cycles of viruses. In 1948, Gertrude created her first compound. It was called diaminopurine and was tested on mice before testing began on humans in 1950. What they eventually found was that diaminopurine was not good enough to completely cure cancer. It was also considered a toxic substance and produced severe side effects, such as intense vomiting.

The drug was tested on patients at Sloan-Kettering Institute in New York. Gertrude watched people take her drug, go into remission, and then relapse and die within two years. This began an emotional roller-coaster ride for Gertrude and Dr. Hitchings, both of whom formed relationships with their patients. Gertrude experienced the same anguish when her patients died as when she lost her grandfather and her fiancé.

One patient in particular had an impact on Gertrude. J. B. was a twenty-three-year-old woman who seemed to recover after taking diaminopurine. She went on to marry and have a child after being treated for her cancer. But two years after believing she had fully recovered, she became sick again and died. Today, J. B. probably would have been given larger doses over a period of time of different drugs and would have been cured. She was given no drugs at all during the two years she was in remission. Gertrude cried for J. B. for a long time.

UNDERSTANDING LEUKEMIA

According to the National Cancer Institute, each year more than 2,000 children and 27,000 adults discover they have leukemia. That is in the United

Continued on page 50

Continued from page 49

States alone. Leukemia is a type of cancer. Cancer is not just one disease. It is actually a group of more than 100 diseases. Cancer has a couple of characteristics. One is that certain cells in the body become abnormal. Another is that the body keeps producing these abnormal cells.

Leukemia is a cancer of the blood cells. Normal blood cells are made up of a fluid called plasma and three types of cells. Each type has a special function. One type are white blood cells. These fight infection. There are also red blood cells, which carry oxygen around the body. The third type, called platelets, form clots to control bleeding. Normal blood cells help to keep a body healthy by cleansing the body and helping wounds to stop bleeding. When leukemia develops, the body produces large amounts of abnormal white blood cells, which do not function properly. In 1950, the goals of the biochemistry department at Burroughs Wellcome were to further the ideals of the company's founders and find cures for serious diseases, such as leukemia.

SUCCESS AND SORROW

In 1950, when Gertrude was thirty-two years old, half of the children who acquired acute leukemia died within a few months. It was during this year that she created 6-mercaptopurine, or 6-MP, the revolutionary drug that would change the death rate of childhood leukemia victims forever. The marketed name (which is what a drug is called when it is sold through prescriptions) was Purinethol. In mice, tumors treated with 6-MP failed to grow. 6-MP brought about longer-lasting results for patients in 1953, but they were still getting sick again. Finally, Gertrude altered the compounds of the chemicals, and she and Dr. Hitchings discovered that 6-MP, when combined with other drugs, could cure different types of leukemia. They had to mix and match.

Today, a combination of 6-MP and other drugs can cure 80 percent of the children who develop leukemia. Realizing the importance of

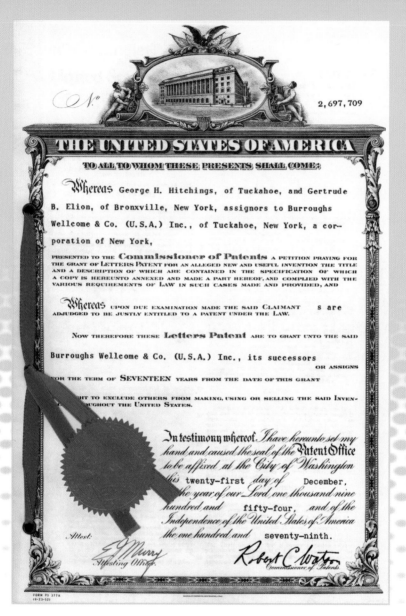

In 1954, Gertrude and Dr. Hitchings were granted a patent for 6-MP, a revolutionary drug that caused complete remission in 40 percent of the children with leukemia at the time

her contribution to medicine, Gertrude stopped caring whether or not she had a Ph.D. She preferred saving lives.

In late 1953, within days of the first patient taking 6-MP and responding well to it, the Food and Drug Administration (FDA) approved 6-MP before even receiving any scientific data on it. (Nowadays, the FDA is much more thorough in its research before approving drugs.)

EXPANDING IDEAS

When Burroughs Wellcome submitted 6-MP compounds to the Sloan-Kettering Institute, 6-MP had produced several remissions in leukemia. The director at the time, C. P. Rhoads, offered Burroughs Wellcome financial support. Dr. Hitchings's team continued to look for antitumor drugs. The financial help also allowed the pharmaceutical company to expand and hire fifteen more people. It was the beginning of a wonderful relationship.

Gertrude tested many of her drug compounds on cancer patients at Sloan-Kettering Institute. This research hospital was founded in 1884 as the cornerstone of the New York Cancer Hospital, which makes it the world's oldest and largest private institute dedicated to cancer education and research.

Gertrude was always asking more questions: "What does this mean?" or "Why did this happen?" Gertrude even worked on weekends at her parents' summer cottage. Her mother, Bertha, thought there was something wrong with her daughter when she *didn't* bring work home.

Gertrude once said the only compliment Dr. Hitchings ever gave her was on a blue suit she wore. Instead of compliments, Hitchings gave her promotions. Gertrude was usually one step behind him at Burroughs Wellcome. Whenever he would leave a position, she would fill it. After the publication of her twentieth paper, however, he helped arrange her membership to the acclaimed and prestigious American Society of Biological Chemists. Now, no one was stopping her. A door to cancer research had been opened.

OTHER ACHIEVEMENTS

In 1952, Gertrude created a drug to treat malaria, an infection of the red blood cells. Malaria can be contracted from the bite of an infected female mosquito, from a blood transfusion using contaminated blood, or from an injection with a needle that was previously used by a person with the infection. It can rapidly damage red blood cells and eventually cause kidney failure. Although malaria is not much of a threat in the United States, Gertrude's cure was used in developing nations and in the rain forests of the world, places where malaria often occurred. The drug was called pyrimethamine, and it was the first antimalaria drug. Daraprim, the brand name of pyrimethamine, was invented at Burroughs Wellcome in 1952.

In the late 1950s, Gertrude also developed trimethoprim, which is called Proloprim and Trimpex, to treat bacterial infections, such as urinary tract infections. All of these drugs are still used today.

Unfortunately, she could not protect the ones she loved from disease. In 1956, her mother, Bertha, too embarrassed to see a physician in the early stages of the illness when it might have been possible to help her, died from cervical cancer. Gertrude did not have the power to cure her. Today, cervical cancer is almost 100 percent curable if detected early. Bertha Elion's death was one of the most painful experiences Gertrude had to go through. Gertrude knew that her mother always secretly wanted to have a fulfilling career, and now her mother would not be able to see her daughter reach her peak of success. Although by this time Gertrude had taken great strides in helping to cure disease, she had not yet reached the pinnacle of her career. Gertrude vowed to work harder and keep finding cures for diseases.

BREAKTHROUGH TRIGGERS BREAKTHROUGH

In 1957, Gertrude synthesized a highly sophisticated version of 6-MP called azathioprine, also known as Imuran. By this time, she had been working with 6-MP for about seven years, trying to understand every element of how it worked. In 1958, a young British scientist, Roy Calne, conducted experiments dealing with transplants on dogs. When Calne stopped by Burroughs Wellcome on his way to complete a fellowship in Boston, he asked Gertrude if he could try out some of 6-MP's relatives, or combinations, that she had been working on. Soon enough, Calne used a vial that Gertrude had given him, marked vial #57-322. This compound allowed for a successful kidney implant into a dog. More precisely, people with different tissues could now participate in organ transplants, making more available to people in need. What was in vial #57-322 that made it possible to transplant kidneys between two unrelated people (or two unrelated dogs in this case)? The drug in vial #57-322 was called Imuran. Imuran also helped with severe arthritis. This drug was kept secret until 1959, when it was used to transplant a foreign kidney into a dog named Lollipop, a collie. The transplant was a complete success. Gertrude and Dr. Hitchings celebrated the success of Lollipop by visiting her. Lollipop had a litter of pups and lived for 230 days more before dying from an unrelated cause. Gertrude also discovered that Imuran treated autoimmune lupus, various anemias, and hepatitis.

In 1954, the first successful kidney transplant took place between identical twins in Boston. And in 1961, the first transplants were tried on unrelated humans with Imuran. They survived. Since 1962, more than 100,000 kidney transplants have been performed in the United States, most with Imuran.

In 1959, Imuran was used in a kidney transplant on a dog named Lollipop. After the operation proved to be a success, Gertrude visited Lollipop at Harvard Medical School. Here with other doctors, she pets the dog that will forever be known as the first to receive a foreign kidney.

Gertrude gave many talks, especially at universities, and one thing she noted, written in *Nobel Prize Women in Science*, was, "When the Nobel Prize came in, everybody said, 'How does it feel to get the Nobel Prize?' And I said, 'It's very nice but that's not what it's all about.' I'm not belittling the prize. The prize has done a lot for me, but if it hadn't happened, it wouldn't have made that much difference . . . When you meet someone who has lived for twenty-five years with a kidney graft, there's your reward." Gertrude was more concerned with helping others recover from their illnesses than her own fame or fortune. Clearly, she valued human life more than any prize.

Even though World War II marked a terrible time of human suffering, it also gave one woman a chance to be one of the greatest humanitarian scientists of her generation.

5

Continuing to Cure

In 1963, Gertrude developed a drug called allopurinol, also known as Zyloprim. This medicine helped treat gout. Gout is one of the most common forms of arthritis. It appears as a severe attack, often coming on overnight. Within twelve to twenty-four hours, there is severe pain and swelling in the affected joint. The skin may look red and shiny. Gout occurs when too much uric acid is built up in the body. Uric acid is a chemical that is a natural part of the normal breaking down and building up of food. It can build up in abnormal amounts because too much is produced or the kidneys are not getting rid of it efficiently. In either case, the uric acid turns into chalky crystals, which may cause painful urinary sores that block the kidneys. It is not only very painful, but it can be fatal. Allopurinol inhibits the formation of uric acid. Before the invention of allopurinol, a total of more than 10,000 gout victims died from kidney blockage in the United States alone each year.

Allopurinol also proved helpful for cancer patients being treated with chemotherapy. Chemotherapy tends to kill cancer tissue very quickly, which makes the body produce more uric acid, thereby making gout a common and unfortunate side effect of this kind of cancer treatment.

Later, scientists discovered that allopurinol works against leishmaniasis disease, which is a disease that exists mostly in the Middle East and North Africa and is any of a group of tropical diseases caused by a parasite that lives in dogs, foxes, rodents, and humans. They also found that allopurinol is effective against Chagas' disease, which is an illness in Central and South America, spread through insect bites, that can be fatal.

DESERVING OF RECOGNITION

Gertrude encouraged department heads at Burroughs Wellcome to pursue finding cures for diseases in South America, despite the fact that at the time, it was probably not an economic gain for the company. Gertrude's interest in these matters showed people that she had a real social conscience outside the laboratory.

Dr. George Hitchings retired in 1967 and, as was the tradition, Gertrude moved right into his position. She was made head of the Department of Experimental Therapy at Burroughs Wellcome. The department had never been led by a woman before. In fact, Gertrude was the first woman to lead a major research group.

Gertrude said in *Scientific American* magazine, "As far as I was concerned, the glass ceiling broke when I was made head of the Department of Experimental Therapy in 1967. I had no Ph.D. When I tried to get one by going to school part time, I was told by the dean of Brooklyn Polytechnic Institute that if I didn't give up the job I loved, I

CURRENT NEWS

GERTRUDE ELION HONORED BY AMERICAN CHEMICAL SOCIETY

Gertrude B. Elion, head of Experimental Therapy in our research laboratories, has won the American Chemical Society's $2000 Garvan Medal. The Garvan Medal was established in 1936 to recognize outstanding U.S. women chemists. The award will be presented to Miss Elion at the 155th national ACS meeting in San Francisco next April.

Most of Miss Elion's work has been in the field of chemotherapy. She is noted for her development of Company drugs for leukemia, tumors and gout. She has published more than 130 technical papers and has received numerous U.S. patents.

Born in New York City, Miss Elion received her A.B. degree summa cum laude from Hunter College in 1937 and her M.S. from New York University in 1941. She was a research assistant in organic chemistry with the Denver Chemical Manufacturing Company, New York, in 1938-39, and taught chemistry and physics in the secondary schools of New York City from 1940 to 1942. After working as a food analyst with the Quaker Maid Company in Brooklyn, she became a research assistant in organic synthesis with Johnson and Johnson in New Brunswick, N.J.

Miss Elion joined 'B.W. & Co.' in 1944 as a biochemist. She became senior research chemist in 1950, and assistant to Dr. Hitchings when he was appointed Associate Research Director in 1955 and Research Director of Chemotherapy in 1963. She assumed her present post this year.

A member of the American Chemical Society since 1945, Miss Elion was secretary of the Westchester Subsection of the Society's New York Section in 1960 and chairman of the subsection the following year. She has served as an alternate representative of the New York Section on the Society's national Council since 1964.

Miss Elion is also a member of the American Association for the Advancement of Science, The Chemical Society (London), the American Society of Biological Chemists, the American Association for Cancer Research, the American Society of Hematology, and the honorary scholastic society Phi Beta Kappa. She is a fellow of the New York Academy of Sciences, and was a consultant for the cancer chemotherapy study section of the U.S. Public Health Service from 1960 to 1964.

After Gertrude won the Garvan Medal in 1969, Burroughs Wellcome announced the good news in its newsletter. Gertrude's many years working for Burroughs Wellcome resulted in the invention of many new drugs. Her work in the lab helped her win many prestigious awards.

obviously wasn't serious about a doctorate . . . That position was more than I ever dreamed of. The idea of obtaining a Ph.D. faded into oblivion."

It was also during this time, in 1968, that Gertrude was given the Garvan Medal from the American Chemical Society. It was a prestigious $2,000 prize, and this definitely gave her a new stamp of approval in the scientific community. Until 1980, it was the only award given to women by the American Chemical Society. Gertrude was so touched by receiving this award that she cried.

A PRESTIGIOUS AWARD

Dr. Francis P. Garvan was president of the Chemical Foundation of America from 1919 to 1937. In 1936, the American Chemical Society established the Francis P. Garvan Medal as an award. The medal is awarded in recognition of significant achievements by women chemists in America. It consists of an inscribed gold medal and an honorarium—a monetary award. In 1984, the Olin Corporation assumed sponsorship of the medal, so today it is called the Garvan-Olin Medal.

ELUSIVE DEGREE NO MORE

Ironically, the doctoral degree that Gertrude had sought so fiercely fell into her lap in 1969 when she received an honorary doctorate from George Washington University. Soon after Gertrude won the Garvan Medal, she got a phone call from George Mandell, a professor at George Washington University. He knew her published papers very well. According to *Nobel Prize Women in Science*, he said, "Look, the kind of work you're doing, you've long since passed what a doctorate [degree] would have meant, but we've got to make an honest woman out of you. We'll give you a doctorate, so we can call you 'doctor' legitimately." Standing on the platform, after receiving the degree, Gertrude thought of her mother, Bertha, and wished she was alive to see what Gertrude had achieved. Bertha had wanted her daughter to have a career so badly and would have been so proud to see that Gertrude had such an incredibly important career.

Gertrude was unable to earn a doctorate degree the typical way because of financial limitations. But her research earned her many honorary degrees. In 1969, she received her first honorary degree from George Washington University. Dr. George Hitchings was there to support her as she received this degree.

MOVING INTO THE SUN

In 1970, Burroughs Wellcome moved to Research Triangle Park in the Piedmont region of North Carolina, and Gertrude moved with them. She crammed a two-story condominium full of her belongings: plants, family pictures, artwork, statues, and travel souvenirs. She kept in touch with her brother's children over the phone and visited them by plane. She kept her subscription to the Metropolitan Opera and flew to New York to see shows whenever she could. Pretty soon the born-and-bred New Yorker fit into her warm southern community. She attended basketball games and took every opportunity to attend classical music concerts. She made friends with her neighbor Cora Himadi, with whom she took trips around the world to places such as Asia, Africa, Europe, and South America.

It was also in North Carolina that Burroughs Wellcome eventually merged with the company Glaxo in 1995. But even before then, there was a research team that had grown in size to 1,500 people.

BIG PAYOFF

In the mid to late 1970s, Gertrude was still hard at work. She was still determined to fight against viruses, even though many scientists considered it a waste of time. Gertrude was still haunted by the memory of J. B. She even returned to studying the same kinds of compounds she had studied long ago, the compounds that fought against viruses but were highly toxic, like diaminopurine.

For about four years, Gertrude and her team studied compounds that had some effect on viruses, particularly the herpes virus. With the assistance of Howard Schaeffer, the head of Burroughs Wellcome's organic chemistry division, she put a smaller sugar molecule in the compounds she had been studying and suddenly it seemed as if the virus was confused and acted differently. In 1977, she developed acyclovir, or Zovirax, with Dr. David Barry, a scientist who lived until January 2002. Zovirax is a safe treatment for shingles, mouth and genital sores due to the herpes virus, Epstein-Barr virus, herpes encephalitis (a fatal brain infection in children), and pseudo-rabies in animals. This medicine was also beneficial because the herpes virus could cause death in patients with other serious illnesses if their immune systems were damaged, such as is the case with leukemia patients, cancer patients, and people with transplanted organs.

Zovirax was introduced to scientists in 1978 at a conference in California. It was a very important discovery, and thirteen posters filled an entire lobby explaining every detail about this new drug, from its conception, or beginning, to how it works, to what it cures. Gertrude's research team (about seventy scientists at this time), had kept acyclovir a secret. That way, when they worked out all of the kinks of the drug, they could make it public and patent it. The patent would give them the rights to the drug and prevent other companies from manufacturing it. Gertrude called Zovirax her fine jewel. It was an enormous breakthrough in antiviral research. It became Burroughs Wellcome's largest selling product, with worldwide sales of $838 million in 1991.

6

Retired and Rewarded

After years of taking her work home with her and going into the lab every day, Gertrude Elion decided to retire from Burroughs Wellcome in 1983. She was sixty-five years old and wanted to travel a bit more outside the laboratory. She remained on staff as a consultant and emerita scientist, or a person who is given an honorary title after retirement. This meant that even though Gertrude was retired, she was still thrilled to go into the laboratory and help any staff member with a problem or give advice on an experiment. Gertrude loved the job so much that it never really left her blood.

Life did not slow down for Gertrude, however. She did indulge herself in her favorite hobbies: traveling and photography. Whenever she had some extra money, she would not spend it on fancy cars or clothes; it was always travel that Gertrude spent her money on. Maybe in some way, she was making up for all of the imaginary trips her father, Robert, had taken.

Gertrude also became a research professor of pharmacology and medicine at Duke University in Durham, North Carolina, and adjunct professor of pharmacology at the University of North Carolina in Chapel Hill. She still loved to teach, and these jobs meant she could still teach students in the classroom even if she was not in an office. Gertrude so thoroughly enjoyed sharing her extensive knowledge with others. Each year she looked forward to mentoring a third-year Duke medical student.

In Mary Ellen Avery's *Biographical Memoirs* from the National Academy of Sciences, Gertrude's nephew (Herbert's son), Jonathan

Gertrude enjoyed working with students. In this photo still taken from a video by Bella Productions, Gertrude mentors a student at Duke University.

Elion, remembered his aunt. He said, "She made herself available to students. While people tell me now she was an advocate to the advancement of women in science, this actually comes as news to me, as I always thought of her as advocating the advancement of ALL persons in science. She was active in the North Carolina School of Medicine and Math, did lots with Duke medical students, loved to have young students visit Burroughs Wellcome (and kept a stack of books about herself directed at kids to give away). When she was a visiting professor at Brown University, she didn't want to meet with the VIPs and department heads, she asked to arrange for time with the students."

CONTINUING HER FIGHT AGAINST DISEASE

After her official retirement from Burroughs Wellcome in 1983, Gertrude went on to work with the World Health Organization (WHO). Founded in 1948, the World Health Organization is a specialized agency of the United Nations with 191 member states that promotes cooperation for health among nations and carries out governmental programs to control and diminish disease.

Gertrude served on several committees of WHO. One was the tropical disease research division, which focused on helping people and preventing malaria, filariasis (a worm infection), and onchocerciasis (also called river blindness, the world's second leading infectious cause of blind-

After retiring from Burroughs Wellcome in 1983, Gertrude went to work for the World Health Organization, serving on the committee for tropical disease research. As part of the World Health Organization, Gertrude researched the effects of chemotherapy on malaria, a disease that affects 40 percent of the world's population, mostly in poor countries.

ness). Gertrude's dedication to WHO helped ensure that her work touched lives around the globe, even those in less developed nations than the United States.

FIGHTING THE MOST INFAMOUS PLAGUE

In 1984, Gertrude's lab used her methodology—her way of thinking—to develop azidothymidine (AZT), a treatment for AIDS (acquired immunodeficiency syndrome). Gertrude's methodology had to do with always using all of the information and knowledge one acquired. If she found a compound or drug that worked, she would try to build on that particular drug, not start from scratch. That would explain why so many of the drugs she developed tied into each other in some way. AZT was approved by the FDA in 1987 and became commercially available. In combination with other drugs, AZT may lower measurements of HIV in one's bloodstream and it is likely to increase one's T-cell, or white blood cell, count. Having a higher white blood cell count helps boost immunity and helps reduce the likelihood of developing other infections. Today, the most effective method of fighting HIV/AIDS is taking AZT with a combination of other drugs.

Gertrude is often credited with the development of AZT, but she said she did not play a direct role. It was her method of looking at things that helped others discover the drug. Gertrude traveled the university circuit, met students, and gave lectures on her career. Gertrude talked about her life and the path she had taken but did not really toot her own horn. Instead, she inspired students to follow their dreams and never give up.

AN IMPORTANT PHONE CALL

On October 17, 1988, at 6:30 AM, Gertrude got a phone call while she was washing her face. It was a reporter, congratulating her on winning the Nobel Prize. Gertrude thought he was joking until he mentioned the other winners along with her: Dr. George Hitchings and Sir James Black. (Sir James

Black discovered two classes of drugs, beta-blockers for high blood pressure and heart disease, and H-2 antagonists for ulcers.) The three of them won the Nobel Prize in Physiology or Medicine "for development of rational method for drug design and discoveries in principles of chemotherapy." Between them, the three shared $390,000. It was the first Nobel Prize for drug research in thirty-one years and one of the very few for cancer treatment in general. At this time, Gertrude was seventy years old and Dr. Hitchings was eighty-three: He was one of the oldest winners in history. Gertrude and Dr. Hitchings won the Nobel Prize because they had created a series of drugs that fought viruses without hurting human cells—something that no other researchers were able to do.

Gertrude wore a blue chiffon gown to the ceremony to accept her Nobel Prize. Everyone else was in black and white. Gertrude brought all of her nieces and nephews, along with their spouses and even their children to the Nobel ceremonies in Stockholm, Sweden. She brought a total of eleven people with her! Four of the children were under the age of five. Gertrude insisted to the officials that the children be able to attend the formal dinner banquet. According to *Nobel Prize Women in Science*, when certain officials were astonished, she said, "I'm not going to bring them all the way to Sweden and then have them spend the evening in a hotel room. You put them at a separate table where they can see their parents and their parents can see them and they'll be fine." The children behaved beautifully and enchanted everyone there, including the press. Gertrude smiled the whole night long and tapped her feet to the beat when the chamber orchestra struck up an aria from Mozart's opera *Don Giovanni*. She thoroughly enjoyed the evening. In her speech, Gertrude mentioned that forty years of research not only created life-saving drugs but also served as a period of time for her to try to uncover the mysteries of nature. She was thrilled to be led down the path of so many arms of research, including pharmacology, immunology, and virology.

FEMALE NOBEL PRIZE WINNERS

Only seven Nobel Prizes in the field of medicine have gone to women in the ninety-seven years the prize has been awarded. Marie Curie (1903 and 1911), Marie Curie's daughter, Irene Joliot-Curie (1935), Dorothy Crowfoot Hodgkin (1964), Barbara McClintock (1983), Rita Levi-Montalcini (1986), and Gertrude Elion (1988) are in a class all their own.

In 1986, Italian neurologist Rita Levi-Montalcini accepted a Nobel Prize for her medical discoveries.

In 1983, Barbara McClintock received an unshared Nobel Prize in Medicine from King Carl Gustaf of Sweden.

MEDALS AND MEETING
THE PRESIDENT

Winning the Nobel Prize thrust Gertrude into the spotlight. She hired a full-time secretary and had a huge office stuffed full of Nobel memorabilia. Gertrude had to cancel a seminar at Tufts University to accept the National Medal of Science from President George H. W. Bush in 1991. The National Medal of Science is the nation's highest science honor, but Gertrude's brother, Herbert, was upset that she had broken a family rule: Never turn down a previous invitation to accept a better one. At the ceremony, President Bush announced that Gertrude had "transformed the world," according to a 1999 *New York Times* article.

Dr. Weiss, Gertrude's classmate from NYU, was listening to the radio in his kitchen when he heard that Gertrude had won the Nobel Prize. He remembered, "I was very happy for her. It was a great accomplishment. After she won, there were two schools in New York that took out full-page ads in the *New York Times*. The ads showed a circle of names of people who had gone to their schools and won Nobel Prizes. Her name was in it."

As a reward for winning the Nobel Prize and for exhibiting such excellence in their company, Burroughs Wellcome gave Dr. Hitchings and Gertrude $250,000 each to donate to charity. Gertrude gave hers to Hunter College for women's fellowships in chemistry and biochemistry. Some colleagues say winning the Nobel Prize strained her relationship with George Hitchings a bit. They were often a little competitive with one another. As Elvira Falco noted in *Nobel Prize Women in Science*, "They worked together as well as any two people worked together. But I have a feeling that when your assistant gets as much credit as you have, it may be a difficult thing."

EXCLUSIVE MEMBERSHIPS

In 1990, Gertrude was finally elected to the National Academy of Sciences. It was Gertrude who started a campaign to get Dr. Hitchings elected in 1975, and now Gertrude herself was being awarded this honor. She was finally step-ping out of Hitchings's shadow.

In 1991, Gertrude was also the first woman inducted into the National Inventors Hall of Fame, (NIHF), the same organization that honored Thomas Edison for his invention of the electric lamp and Alexander Graham Bell for his invention of the telephone. The NIHF honors the men and women responsible for technological advances that make progress possible. Each year, the selection com-mittee of the NIHF Foundation selects inven-tors for induction. The committee includes repre-sentatives from the leading scientific organizations.

Gertrude was also inducted into the National Women's Hall of Fame in Seneca Falls, New York, in 1991, for her achievements in sci-ence. The National Women's Hall of Fame honors American women every year for their contribu-tions to society. Gertrude joined a group of women that included Elizabeth Blackwell, the first woman to earn an M.D. degree, and Sally Ride, the first female American astronaut.

And the awards kept coming. In 1997, when Gertrude was seventy-nine years old, the Lemelston-MIT Prize Program, administered by the Massachusetts Institute of Technology, gave Gertrude a lifetime achievement award. By this time, Gertrude also held forty-five patents for the numerous life-saving drugs she had created between 1944 and 1983. The ceremony took place April 10, 1997, at the Smithsonian National Museum of American History in Washington, D.C. Inventor Jerome Lemelson and his wife, Dorothy, established the Lemelson-MIT Prize Program at MIT in 1994 to recognize the country's most talented inventors and to create role models for America's youth. According to the Lemelson-MIT Awards Program Web site, http://web.mit.edu/invent, Charles M. Vest, president of MIT, said at the ceremony, "She deserves acclaim not only for her achievements as a research chemist but also for her devoted and inspirational mentoring of young students, and especially young women."

GERTRUDE ELION

In 1995, Gertrude was the winner of the Higuchi Memorial Award and lectured at the University of Kansas. Gertrude continued to travel and lecture. She did not want to stop until, as her nephew Jonathan put it, "she was all used up."

7

Looking Back

With regard to giving advice, in *Scientific American* magazine, Gertrude said, "What advice can I give women today? I have no mysterious secrets to impart. The most important advice is to choose the field that makes you happiest. There is nothing better than loving your work. Second, set a goal for yourself. Even if it is an 'impossible dream,' each step toward it gives a feeling of accomplishment. Finally, be persistent. Don't let yourself be discouraged by others, and believe in yourself."

As Elvira Falco noticed, Gertrude's relationship with Dr. Hitchings was strained for a bit after they won the Nobel Prize.

Gertrude had finally shown the world how important her contributions were, and she was not standing in anyone's shadow any longer. Gertrude acknowledged that they had their differences for years, but their work was intricately tied together. People at Burroughs Wellcome could never tell which contribution on a scientific paper was hers and which was from Dr. Hitchings. When describing their work, Gertrude might have used "we" more often than "I," whereas with Dr. Hitchings, it was the opposite. He preferred to take credit for their combined contributions. She did remember, "He never paid me a compliment! . . . He perceives that he started it all . . . But actually he was always willing to listen to [a] suggestion. I said I wanted to study metabolism . . . He just let us do what we thought we should be doing," according to *Nobel Prize Women in Science*.

A LONG LIFE

One February morning, Gertrude went for a walk, but she never returned home. She collapsed and

Gertrude poses with one of her lab notebooks. She recorded her research in handwritten accounts of her experiments, including the discovery of 6-MP. Gertrude was the first woman inducted into the National Inventors Hall of Fame and won a lifetime achievement award from the Lemelson-MIT Prize Program.

was taken to Chapel Hill's University of North Carolina Hospital. She died at midnight on February 21, 1999. She was eighty-one years old. Until her death, Gertrude had continued to teach at Duke University in North Carolina. Even though she had retired, she was still working every day.

Gertrude was involved with the board of directors of the Burroughs Wellcome Fund (BWF), a private foundation based in North Carolina that is dedicated to advancing medical studies. The BWF created the Gertrude B. Elion Mentored Medical Student Research Award following her death. This award is administered through the Triangle Community Foundation in her honor and, more important, will support female medical students interested in pursuing health-related research projects. Two awards of $12,500 each are presented annually to increase opportunities in the medical field for women. Nominations for the award can be submitted at any one of the four medical schools in North Carolina: Duke, East Carolina University,

During Gertrude's retirement years, she taught as a research professor at Duke University School of Medicine. Although Gertrude never earned her Ph.D., which is a requirement to teach at the graduate level, she received twenty-five honorary degrees throughout her life.

University of North Carolina at Chapel Hill, and Wake Forest University Baptist Medical Center. Each medical center may nominate up to two women who are enrolled as full-time students, and a committee of distinguished scientists reviews applications. Even after her death, Gertrude continues her legacy of helping others. Although she can no longer teach her students scientific formulas, the Gertrude B. Elion Mentored Medical Student Research Award will carry on her mission to help students further their education.

Gertrude's death was a shock to many. She had touched so many lives and had many grateful admirers. As recorded in the *Biographical Memoirs* by Mary Ellen Avery, Gertrude's nephew Jonathan stated, "The day after she died, I was sorting through her mail. There were two letters that struck me as representative. One was from a university president thanking her for being a visiting professor there. The other was from a young girl . . . The girl talked excitedly about a school project in which they were doing a wax museum, and the students would play the wax figures. She had researched scientists on the Internet and had selected Trudy as her heroine."

IMMORTALIZED

In her lifetime, Gertrude won a large number of awards, including the Medal of Honor from the American Cancer Society; the National Medal of Science; the President's Medal from Hunter College; the City of Medicine Award in Durham, North Carolina; the Lemelson-MIT Lifetime Achievement Award; the Judd Award from Memorial Sloan-Kettering Institute; the Ernst W. Bertner Memorial Award from M. D. Anderson Cancer Center; and the Garvan Medal from the American Chemical Society. What does all this mean? It means that Gertrude's impact on science and medicine was far reaching and her contributions were very significant.

One of the ways in which Gertrude has been immortalized is in an hour-long biographical documentary produced by Bella International Productions, Inc., called *The Living Legacy of Gertrude Elion.* This documentary shows Gertrude's vivacious personality; Gertrude shares anecdotes about her life and experiences. She talks about her parents, her childhood, her struggle during and after school, her experiences at Burroughs Wellcome, and the exciting awards bestowed on her after she retired. Footage from this documentary can be viewed online at the Jewish Women's Archive Web site: http://www.jwa.org.

MOST EXCELLENT HUMANIST

The memory of Gertrude Belle Elion will live on through all of the lives she saved and through the individuals she mentored, taught, and lectured. The first half of her life was devoted to research, and the second half to passing on her knowledge and dedication to other scientists. According to *Gertrude Elion: Master Chemist*, a book written by Stephanie St. Pierre, Gertrude stated a few years before her death, "I've reached a stage where I can teach and I'm ready to pass the research torch on to others to carry." Gertrude wanted to share her knowledge with others; she wanted to inspire her students to get involved in research. She was unselfish in her pursuits.

Through her entire life, Gertrude was always unpretentious, dedicated, and kind to others. Later in her life, she strove to cure diseases as much as she had immediately after the deaths of her grandfather, her fiancé, her mother, and her friend J. B. Her work as a humanist will be remembered as well as her zest for life and compassion for others less fortunate. Her medicines are still used today to cure people of diseases, and her methodology has paved the way for the invention of other important medicines. Through it all, she never let anyone get in the way of achieving her goals. She will be remembered for years to come as a scientist, inventor, teacher, and trailblazer.

TIMELINE

1918   Gertrude Belle Elion is born in New York City on January 23.

1929   Gertrude's father, Robert Elion, is forced to declare bankruptcy because of financial losses due to the stock market crash. Gertrude feels the burden years later when there is not enough money for her to attend college.

1933   Gertrude's grandfather dies painfully of stomach cancer, inspiring Gertrude to pursue a career in science.

1937   Gertrude graduates with highest honors from Hunter College in New York. She works several jobs to earn enough money to enroll at New York University to get her master's degree.

1938   Unable to find a job, Gertrude volunteers at a chemistry lab.

1941   Gertrude receives her M.S. in chemistry from New York University. Gertrude's fiancé, Leonard Canter, dies of a heart infection.

1942   Due to the number of men called off to World War II, Gertrude is able to find a job as a food chemistry analyst.

1944	Gertrude begins work at the Burroughs Wellcome pharmaceutical company during the first week in June. She will stay with Burroughs Wellcome for thirty-nine years.
1950	Gertrude develops the drug 6-mercaptopurine (Purinethol, or 6-MP), which proves to be beneficial in the treatment of childhood leukemia when used with other drugs.
1959	Organ transplants are revolutionized when Gertrude develops Imuran, which allows transplants to take place between tissues of unrelated people.
1967	Gertrude becomes the first woman to lead a research group when she is named head of the Department of Experimental Therapy at Burroughs Wellcome.
1969	Gertrude receives an honorary doctorate from George Washington University, the first of over twenty honorary degrees.
1970	Burroughs Wellcome relocates to North Carolina, and Gertrude moves into a two-story condominium where she will live for the rest of her life.

1977	Acyclovir, or Zovirax, the first medicine to treat viruses, is created in Gertrude's lab.
1983	Gertrude retires from Burroughs Wellcome but stays on as a consultant.
1984	Gertrude's lab uses her methodology to develop AZT, the only drug licensed to treat AIDS until 1991.
1988	Gertrude receives the Nobel Prize in physiology and medicine with George Hitchings and James Black for development of a rational method for drug design and discoveries in the principles of chemotherapy.
1990	Gertrude is elected to the National Academy of Sciences.
1991	The National Medal of Science, the United States's highest honor in science, is awarded to Gertrude. She is also inducted into the Women's Hall of Fame in Seneca Falls, New York.
1999	Gertrude Elion dies on February 21, in North Carolina.

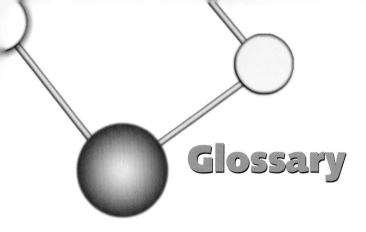

Glossary

anti-Semitic Having hostility or prejudice toward Jewish people.

arthritis A medical condition in which the cartilage between joints in the body dissolves, making bone movements very painful.

bankruptcy The state of having no money; having lost all of one's money.

chemist A person who investigates the composition and properties of chemical substances.

chemotherapy A treatment for cancer that uses harsh chemicals to treat the disease.

compound A distinct substance formed by the chemical union of two or more ingredients.

DNA (deoxyribonucleic acid) A nucleic acid that contains the body's genetic information.

foreclosure A legal proceeding that ends an owner's rights to an estate or property.

ghetto An area where a minority group is sectioned off and forced to live.

hepatitis The inflammation of the liver.

lupus A recurring, chronic disorder characterized by red, round patches on the skin that leave scars.

nucleic acid A macromolecule made from nucleotides. DNA and RNA are nucleic acids. Nucleic acids are used by the body to store genetic information.

patent An official document that secures an inventor (for a term of years) the exclusive rights to use, make, or sell an invention.

persecution The act of causing suffering.

pharmacology The scientific study of drugs and how they work.

rabbi A Jewish person who is knowledgeable about Jewish law; usually the leader of a Jewish congregation.

reagent A substance, which because of the reaction it causes, is used in synthesis.

synthesize To put something together. In chemistry, synthesizing means putting together new molecules.

toxic Of or relating to a poison.

Yiddish A German language written in Hebrew characters that is spoken by Jews and descendants of Jews of central and eastern European origin.

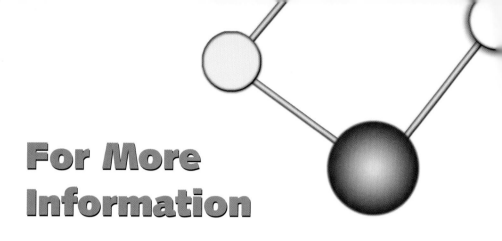

For More Information

American Chemical Society
1155 Sixteenth Street NW
Washington, DC 20036
(800) 227-5558
e-mail: help@acs.org
Web site: http://www.acs.org

Association for Women in Science
1200 New York Avenue NW, Suite 650
Washington, DC 20005
(202) 326-8940
Web site: http://www.awis.org

Jewish Women's Archive
68 Harvard Street
Brookline, MA 02445
(617) 232-2258
Web site: http://www.jwa.org

The National Inventors Hall of Fame
221 South Broadway
Akron, OH 44308-1505
(330) 762-4463
Web site: http://www.invent.org

The National Women's Hall of Fame
76 Fall Street
P.O. Box 335
Seneca Falls, NY 13148
(315) 568-8060
Web site: http://www.greatwomen.org

Women in Technology International
6345 Balboa Boulevard, Suite 257
Encino, CA 91316
(800) 334-9484
Web site: http://www.witi.org

GERTRUDE ELION

WEB SITES

Due to the changing nature of Internet links, the Rosen Publishing Group, Inc., has developed an online list of Web sites related to the subject of this book. This site is updated regularly. Please use this link to access the list:

http://www.rosenlinks.com/whfms/geli/

For Further Reading

Ambrose, Susan A., et al. *Journeys of Women in Science and Engineering: No Universal Constants.* Philadelphia: Temple University Press, 1997.

McGrayne, Sharon Bertsch. *Nobel Prize Women in Science: Their Lives, Struggles & Momentous Discoveries.* Secaucus, NJ: Carol Publishing Group, 1998.

Vare, Ethlie Ann, et al. *Patently Female: From AZT to TV Dinners: Stories of Women Inventors and Their Breakthrough Ideas.* New York: John Wiley & Sons, 2002.

Wasserman, Elga. *The Door in the Dream: Conversations with Eminent Women in Science.* Washington, DC: Joseph Henry Press, 2000.

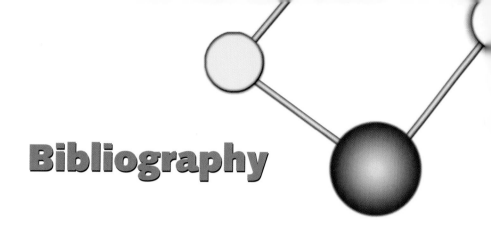

Bibliography

Altman, Lawrence K. "Gertrude Elion, Drug Developer, Dies at 81." *The New York Times*, February 23, 1999, Section A, p. 21.

Ambrose, Susan A., et al. *Journeys of American Women in Science and Engineering: No Universal Constants.* Philadelphia: Temple University Press, 1997.

Avery, Mary Ellen. National Academy of Sciences. "Biographical Memoirs: Gertrude B. Elion." May 1997. Retrieved March 4, 2002 (http://www.nap.edu/html/biomems/gelion.html).

Brokaw, Tom. *The Greatest Generation.* New York: Random House, Inc., 1998.

Bibliography

Elion, Gertrude B. The Nobel Foundation. "Gertrude
   B. Elion—Autobiography." June 20, 2002. Retrieved
   March 9, 2002 (http://www.nobel.se/medicine/lau-
   reates/1988/elion-autobio.html).

Jewish Women's Archive. "Women of Valor: Gertrude
   Elion." Retrieved February 25, 2002
   (http://www.jwa.org/exhibits/elion).

Lemelson-MIT's Program: Invention Dimension.
   "Gertrude Belle Elion." February 28, 1996. Retrieved
   March 14, 2001 (http://web.mit.edu/invent/www/
   inventorsA-H/elion.html).

McGrayne, Sharon Bertsch. *Nobel Prize Women in
   Science: Their Lives, Struggles & Momentous
   Discoveries*. Secaucus, NJ: Carol Publishing
   Group, 1998.

St. Pierre, Stephanie. *Gertrude Elion: Master Chemist*.
   Vero Beach, FL: Rourke Enterprises, Inc, 1993.

Index

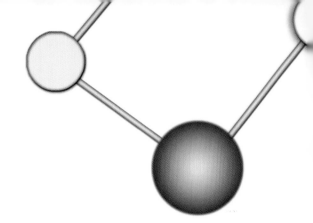

A

acyclovir (Zovirax), 69, 70
AIDS, 8, 76, 77
allopurinol (Zyloprim), 61, 62
American Cancer Society, 93
American Chemical Society, 65, 93
American Society of Biological
    Chemists, 55
anemias, 58
Austro-Hungarian Empire, 12
autoimmune lupus, 58
azathioprine (Imuran), 57–58
azidothymidine (AZT), 76–77

B

Barry, Dr. David, 69
biochemistry, definition of, 39
Biographical Memoirs, excerpts
    from, 72–74, 92–93
Black, Sir James, 77–78
Blackwell, Elizabeth, 84
Burroughs, Silas, 39
Burroughs Wellcome, history of, 39
Burroughs Wellcome Fund, 90
Bush, President George H. W., 82

C

Calne, Roy, 57
Canter, Leonard (fiancé), 9, 31,
    49, 95
Chagas' disease, 62
chemotherapy, 62, 78
City of Medicine Award, 93
Curie, Marie, 7, 16, 80

D

Denver Chemical Company, 27
diaminopurine, 48, 49, 69
DNA, 45
Duke University, 72, 90

E

Elion, Bertha (Cohen), 13, 15–16,
    54, 56, 66, 95
Elion, Gertrude
    awards given to, 65, 77, 82,
        85–86, 93
    at Burroughs Wellcome, 10,
        35–44, 45–47, 48–60,
        61–70, 71
    childhood of, 14–20

and college/graduate school, 21–22, 23, 25–26, 27–28, 44–45
death of, 88–90
drugs developed by, 8, 48, 51, 55–56, 57–58, 61, 69, 76–77
early jobs of, 27–28, 33–34, 35
fiancé and marriage, 9, 28–33, 49, 95
honorary degrees given to, 45, 46, 66
life after retirement, 72, 74–76
relationship with/death of grandfather, 9, 17–18, 24, 49, 95
winning of Nobel Prize, 59–60, 77–79, 82–83
with World Health Organization, 74–76
Elion, Herbert, 18–20, 23, 31, 33, 68, 72, 82
Elion, Jonathan, 72–74, 86, 92–93
Elion, Robert, 13–14, 15, 20, 21, 24, 35, 72
Epstein-Barr virus, 69
Ernst W. Bertner Memorial Award, 93

F

Falco, Elvira, 43, 44, 83, 87
filariasis, 74
Food and Drug Administration, 53, 76

G

Garvan, Dr. Francis P., 65
Garvan Medal (Garvan-Olin Medal), 65, 66, 93
germ theory of disease, 16–17

Gertrude B. Elion Mentored Medical Student Research Award, 90–92
Gertrude Elion: Master Chemist, excerpt from, 94–95
Glaxo, 68
gout, 61–62
Great Depression, 19–20
Greatest Generation, The, excerpt from, 33

H

hepatitis, 58
herpes encephalitis, 69–70
herpes virus/viral herpes, 8, 69, 70
Higuchi Memorial Award, 86
Himadi, Cora, 68
Hitchings, Dr. George, 10, 37, 41–42, 43, 44, 45–47, 48, 49, 51, 53, 54–55, 58, 63, 77, 78, 83, 87–88
Hodgkin, Dorothy Crowfoot, 80
honorary degrees, explanation of, 46
Hoover, President Herbert, 19
Hunter College, 22, 23, 25, 83, 93

I

immunology, definition of, 39

J

J.B., 9, 49, 69, 95
Jewish immigration to America (1870–1918), 12–13
Johnson & Johnson, 35
Joliot-Curie, Irene, 80
Journeys of Women in Science and Engineering, excerpt from, 32
Judd Award, 93

L

leishmaniasis, 62
Lemelson, Jerome and Dorothy, 85
Lemelson-MIT Prize
    Program/Lifetime
    Achievement Award,
    85, 93
leukemia, 8, 9, 10, 41, 44, 51, 53, 70
    explanation of, 49–50
Levi-Montalcini, Rita, 80
Living Legacy of Gertrude Elion,
    The, 94
Lollipop, 58

M

malaria, 8, 37, 55–56, 74
Mandell, George, 66
Massachusetts Institute of
    Technology, 85
McClintock, Barbara, 80
M.D. Anderson Cancer Center, 93
Medal of Honor, 93
Microbe Hunters, 17

N

National Academy of Sciences,
    72, 83
National Cancer Institute, 49
National Defense Research
    Committee, 37
National Inventors Hall of
    Fame, 84
National Medal of Science, 82, 93
National Women's Hall of
    Fame, 84
New Jersey Association for
    Biomedical Research,
    quote from, 24
New York University, 13, 27, 29,
    30, 82

Nobel Prize winners, female, 80
Nobel Prize Women in Science,
    excerpts from, 16, 21–22,
    27, 31, 37, 44, 59–60, 66,
    79, 83, 88
nucleic acids, 45–46

O

Olin Corporation, 65
onchocerciasis, 74–76
opera, 11, 15, 43, 68
organic chemistry, definition of, 39
organ/kidney transplants, 8,
    57–58, 70
Otis, Dr., 25–26

P

Pasteur, Louis, 16–17
penicillin, 31
pharmacologist/pharmacology,
    definitions of, 8, 39
Phi Beta Kappa, 26
photography, 11, 72
Polytechnic Institute (Brooklyn,
    NY), 45
President's Medal from Hunter
    College, 93
pseudo-rabies, 70
pyrimethamine (Daraprim),
    55–56

Q

Quaker Maid Company, 33

R

Rhoads, C. P., 53
Ride, Sally, 84
Russell, Peter, 43, 44
Russia, 12

S

Schaeffer, Howard, 69
Scientific American, excerpts
    from, 63–65, 87
shingles, 69
6-mercaptopurine/6-MP
    (Purinethol),
    51–53, 57
Sloan-Kettering Institute,
    48, 53, 93
stock market crash of 1929, 19, 21
subacute bacterial
    endocarditis, 31

T

trimethoprim (Proloprim/
    Trimpex), 56

U

University of North Carolina in
    Chapel Hill, 72, 92
uric acid, 61–62

V

Vest, Charles M., 85
virology, definition of, 39

W

Weiss, Dr. Philip, 29–30, 82–83
Wellcome, Henry, 39
World Health Organization,
    74–76
World War I, 13
World War II, 9, 36–37, 60

GERTRUDE ELION

ABOUT THE AUTHOR
Jennifer MacBain resides in Manhattan with C. Neil Stephens, her new husband, and their cat, Pixley. Her favorite chemistry experiment was in the third grade when she watched her grandfather show the presence of oxygen and carbon dioxide with a test tube, a candle, some dry ice, and a solution of calcium chloride.

PHOTO CREDITS
Cover and background image © PhotoDisc/Getty Images; cover inset and pp. 38, 40, 59, 89 courtesy of GlaxoSmithKline Heritage Center; pp. 14, 25, 52, 64, 67 courtesy of the Estate of Gertrude Elion; p. 17 © Hulton Archive/Getty Images; pp. 18, 32 courtesy of Jewish Women's Archive; pp. 19, 81 © Bettmann/ Corbis; pp. 36, 54 © Culver Pictures; p. 42 © Will and Deni Mcintyre/Timepix; p. 73 courtesy of Bella International Productions, Inc.; p. 75 www.who.int/ tdr; p. 80 © Arici/Grazia NERI/Corbis Sygma; p. 91 © Steve Vidler/SuperStock.

DESIGN AND LAYOUT
Evelyn Horovicz

EDITOR
Eliza Berkowitz